EMBROIDERY DESIGNS

Classic Creations

KELLY FLETCHER

Everything you need to stitch 12 lettering patterns

becker&mayer! books

Brimming with creative inspiration, how-to projects, and useful information to enrich your everyday life, Quarto Knows is a favorite destination for those pursuing their interests and passions. Visit our site and dig deeper with our books into your area of interest: Quarto Creates, Quarto Cooks, Quarto Homes, Quarto Lives, Quarto Drives, Quarto Explores, Quarto Gifts, or Quarto Kids.

First published in 2017 by becker&mayer books,
an imprint of The Quarto Group.
11120 NE 33rd Place, Suite 101 Bellevue, Washington 98004.
www.QuartoKnows.com

This book is part of the *Embroidery Designs: Classic Creations* kit and is not to be sold separately.

becker&mayer! books titles are also available at discount for retail, wholesale, promotional, and bulk purchase. For details, contact the Special Sales Manager by email at specialsales@quarto.com or by mail at The Quarto Group, Attn: Special Sales Manager, 401 Second Avenue North, Suite 310, Minneapolis, MN 55401 USA.

17 18 19 20 21   5 4 3 2 1

ISBN: 978-0-7603-5519-0

Library of Congress Cataloging-in-Publication Data available upon request.

Author: Kelly Fletcher
Interior Design: Sarah Baynes; Package Design: Megan Sugiyama
Editorial: Leah Jenness
Production: Cindy Curren

Printed, manufactured, and assembled in Hui Zhou, Guangdong, China, 06/17.

Image Credits: White fabric © aopsan/Shutterstock; Stitched ribbon © Ksusha Dusmikeeva/Shutterstock; Burlap background © Maceofoto/Shutterstock; Floral pattern © tets/Shutterstock; Vintage tailor labels and emblems © Ivan Barano/Shutterstock; Embroidery hoop © Geo-grafika/Shutterstock; Background pattern © Maaike Boot/Shutterstock.

171028

Contents

Introduction 5

How to Use This Kit 7

Introduction

Welcome to the *Sew Cute Embroidery Kit!* In these pages, you'll find a basic introduction to hand embroidery stitches, as well as instructions for making each of the adorable designs featured in this kit. Whether you're a brand-new beginner or a seasoned stitcher, there's something for you in these pages.

In hand embroidery, the process is just as important as the end result, so try to stay focused and in the moment while you work. Remember that hand embroidery is seldom perfect. While it's natural to strive for neat stitching, it shouldn't be at the expense of enjoyment.

In addition to the detailed advice on using hoops and needles later in this book, there are a few pointers you can follow that will make you more comfortable while you work and help you achieve better results.

Most important is good light. It prevents eye strain, and because you can see better, your embroidery is automatically neater. Find a stitching spot that has nice natural light or use a lamp with a daylight bulb.

The style of embroidery featured here is easier to do when you can rest your hoop-holding hand against something. Sit either at a table or with a plump cushion on your lap.

Remember to get up every now and again to stretch. It's easy to become absorbed in your work and sit in the same position for hours, but you'll be able to embroider for longer stretches of time if you give your back, neck, and shoulders regular breaks.

The most important thing: Remember to have fun!

How to Use This Kit

Your Kit Contains

Three sheets of iron-on transfers for twelve embroidery projects

Two needles

A 6-inch embroidery hoop

Two pieces of white cotton fabric

Ten skeins of six-stranded embroidery floss

Iron-On Transfers

The iron-on transfers allow you to put an image or outline onto fabric using a hot iron. The images on the transfers here are reversed so they will appear the right way around on the fabric. A design should transfer several times. Generally, the longer you iron the design, the darker the lines. The ink may fade with washing, but this is not guaranteed.

To transfer an image, cut out the design from the sheet, or transfer the whole design as is.

Place the transfer facedown on the fabric and press the back firmly with a dry hot iron for 5 to 10 seconds. Avoid sliding the iron along the back; rather, lift it gently and reposition.

Raise a corner of the transfer paper to check that the design appears on the fabric before removing the transfer paper completely.

Needles

Two types of needles to use in your embroidery are included in this kit:

- *Embroidery needle:* Sometimes called crewel needles, embroidery needles have a fairly large, long eye to make them easier to thread. They come in various sizes. Your thread should pull easily through the eye, but not so much so that it slips out while you're stitching.

- *Milliner needle:* Milliners are also known as straw needles. They are the same width from eye to tip, making them ideal for knots, as they pull easily through the wrapped thread.

Use the embroidery needle for everything other than French knots and pistil stitches. For those, use the milliner needle.

Hoop & Fabric

An embroidery hoop keeps your fabric taut and helps stop it from puckering as you stitch.

Place the smaller hoop on a flat surface. Lay your fabric over the top, with the section of the design you'll embroider centered in the hoop. Loosen the screw in the bigger hoop just enough to allow the hoop to slip over the fabric and sandwich the material between it and the bottom hoop. Pull the fabric as tight as possible in the hoop without distorting the lines of the design, then tighten the screw. The fabric will loosen as you stitch, so you'll have to tighten it again periodically.

Don't be afraid to move your hoop around as you work. You need to be able to work the stitches comfortably for the best results. The embroidery will survive a bit of squashing—just pinch it back into place afterward. Try to avoid squishing knots if you can, though. It's helpful to leave them to do last.

Threads

Embroidery threads are made of six strands twisted into one thread, which you can split back into strands as needed. Cut a length of thread, generally about 16 inches (or 40 cm). Divide it into the number of strands you need at one end, then slide a finger between the strands and down the length of the thread to separate them.

For stitches such as back, blanket, satin, and straight, split the thread into individual strands and then group them together again before threading your needle. This gives the stitches a smoother look, as the strands lie neatly alongside one another. For stem, chain, and other stitches where the individual strands aren't as visible, separating strands is optional.

Six-stranded thread has a natural twist to it, but it can twist too tightly as you work and leave your stitches looking thin and scraggly. To loosen the thread a bit, spin your needle between your thumb and forefinger, or turn your hoop upside down and let your needle dangle—the thread will uncoil naturally.

Optional: Backing Fabric

Attaching a piece of cotton voile or finely woven muslin fabric to the back of your embroidery or ground fabric will help stabilize it while you stitch and give you additional options for securing your thread before starting to embroider.

Stitching

Step-by-Step

On the following pages, you'll find step-by-step instructions and reference photos for the basic embroidery stitches you'll use to make the designs in this kit and beyond.

☀ *A note for lefties: Left-handed embroiderers can turn the book upside down or look at how to do the stitches in a mirror as a makeshift solution. But if you intend to or already do a fair amount of embroidery, investing in a stitch book for left-handed embroiderers can save you hours of mental anguish.*

How to Start and End Threads

To prevent your embroidery stitches from coming undone, you need to secure the start and end of each thread. Ways of doing this depend on personal preference and the stitch you intend to use. For example, use a knot when the lump it may make underneath the fabric won't be visible—like when embroidering French knots. End off each thread as you finish stitching to secure it and cut off any excess so it won't get tangled in your working thread.

Here are some methods for starting and ending threads:

Waste knot: For this temporary knot, knot the end of your thread, and then take the thread to the back of the fabric, about 3 or 4 inches away from where you're going to make your first stitch. Bring the thread to the front again to start embroidering. When done, cut the knot off  and thread away on the back as you would to end off.

Double stitch: If you're using backing fabric, make a small double stitch through the backing fabric only, underneath the section you're about to embroider. Then bring the thread to the front and begin stitching. Cut off any excess thread.

Knot: Hold the tail end of your thread as well as the eye end of the needle between your thumb and forefinger, and wrap the thread around the needle two or three times. Holding the thread taut in your other hand, pull the wraps of thread up the needle and under your thumb and forefinger holding the eye end. Pull the needle through the loops to make a neat knot. Insert the needle directly below where you want to start to embroider.

Finishing off: End off a row by taking your thread to the back of the fabric and securing it under the stitching. You are, in effect, whipping the back of the stitching (see Whipped Chain Stitch on p. 21). Secure it under a few stitches, at least five, or more if necessary. You can also knot the thread, keeping it as close to the back of the fabric as possible, or make a small double stitch if you've used backing fabric.

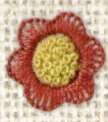

Straight Stitch

The straight stitch is also known as an isolated satin stitch or stroke stitch. This simple stitch forms the basis of many other stitches, so it's covered first.

THE STEPS

1. Come up at A and take your needle down again at B.

2. Pull the thread through until the stitch lies neatly on top of the fabric.

3. Straight stitches arranged in a circle or starburst pattern are sometimes referred to as ray or spoke stitches (see the flower design on p. 53).

Backstitch

The backstitch is good for lines and outlines, especially those with a lot of sharp points. It can be structured in various ways to interesting effect—for example, to create a trellis.

THE STEPS

——————— ✕ ———————

1. Bring the thread to the front of the fabric at A. Stick your needle into the fabric at B (the start of the line) and out again at C to create the first stitch.

2. To end the row, take your needle to the back of the fabric at D.

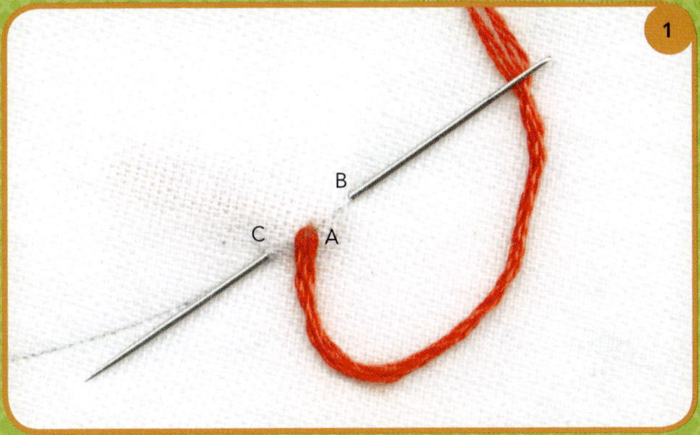

1

B

C A

2

D

Backstitch Trellis

To create a backstitch trellis, embroider intersecting rows of backstitch in a grid pattern in such a way that the stitches start and end at the intersections (see the Planted Flower design on p. 60).

Blanket Stitch

When the stitches are worked close together, blanket stitch is called buttonhole stitch. The purl edge is the solid line along the bottom edge of the stitches. It's a versatile stitch that was originally used to edge blankets and can be embroidered in a circle to create pinwheels.

THE STEPS

1. Bring the thread up at A. Stick the needle into the fabric at B and reemerge at C, keeping the thread under the tip of the needle.

2. Take the needle to the back of the fabric at D to end a row, catching down the last blanket stitch.

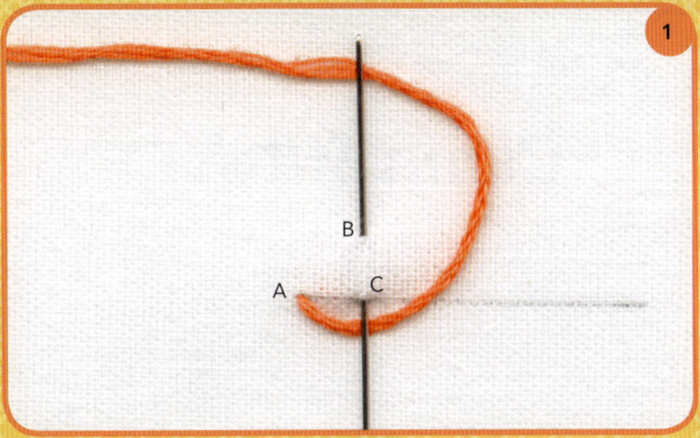

1

B
A   C

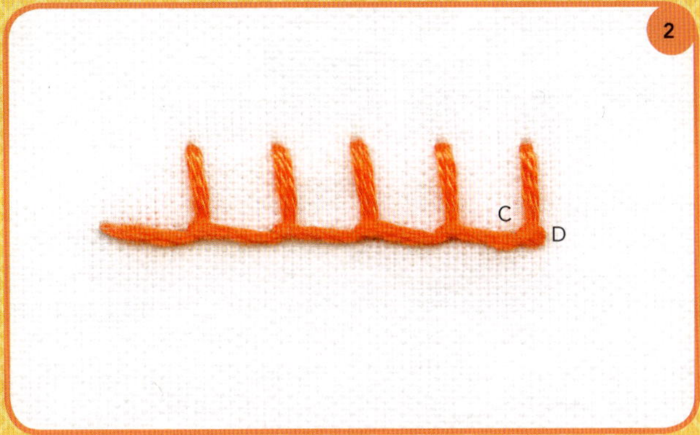

2

C
D

Blanket Stitch Pinwheels

To create a blanket stitch pinwheel, insert the needle into the fabric at B each time and stitch around the circle. For the last stitch, take your needle down at B and reemerge at A (through the same hole). Take the thread to the back again at C—rather than catching down the last stitch—to hide the join. Pinwheels can be stitched with open or closed centers.

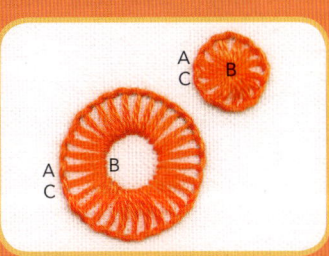

Chain Stitch

Chain stitch can be used for outlines as well as in rows to fill or partially fill a shape. And it can be whipped in a similar or contrasting color thread to create a new stitch.

THE STEPS

1. Bring the thread up at A and then take your needle back down through A and reemerge at B, keeping the thread under the tip of the needle. Pull the thread through until the first chain stitch is neatly looped around the emerging thread. Be careful not to pull too tightly or the stitch will distort. For the second and consecutive chain stitches, take the needle back in at B and reemerge at C.

2. To end off a row, make a small securing stitch by taking the thread down at D. To end off a closed shape such as a circle, come up at C and then slide your needle under the top of the first chain to create a mock chain stitch before taking your thread back down through C.

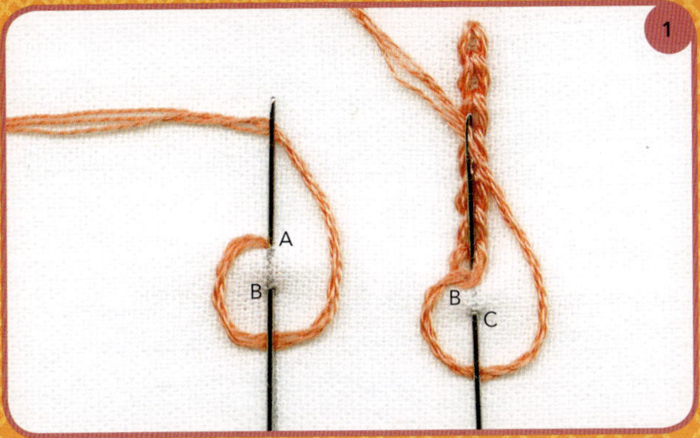

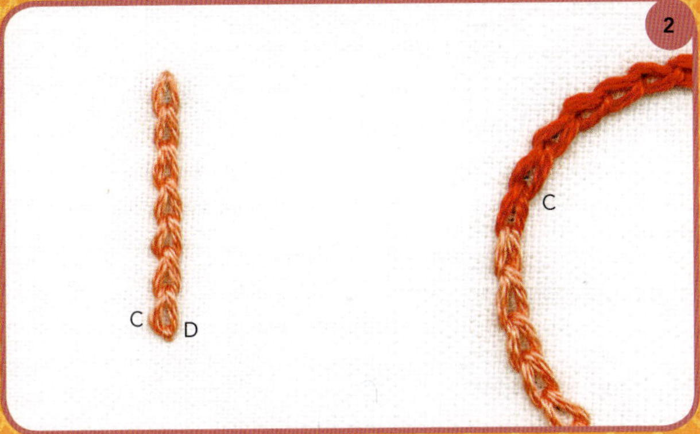

Whipped Chain Stitch

Bring your thread to the front at E. Slide the needle under the second chain stitch in the row, from right to left, without piercing the fabric. Whip the whole row or a section of the row of chain stitches in this way. To end off, take your thread to the back to the right of the last chain stitch.

Cross-Stitch

Cross-stitch is probably the most familiar embroidery stitch. It can be worked as an isolated stitch or in rows. The four points of each cross-stitch should form a square.

THE STEPS

1. Bring your thread up at A and down at B to create the first half of the cross.

2. Bring the needle up at C and take it down again at D to complete the stitch.

3. Pull the thread through until the cross lies neatly on the fabric.

Detached Chain Stitch

Detached chain stitches are simply isolated chain stitches. They can be stitched along a line or arranged in rows to fill an area of a design. They make excellent flower petals and leaves.

THE STEPS

1. Bring the thread up at A and then take your needle back down through A and reemerge at B, keeping the thread under the tip of the needle. Pull the thread through until the chain stitch is neatly looped around the emerging thread. Be careful not to pull too tightly or the stitch will distort.

2. Take the thread back down at C to complete the detached chain stitch.

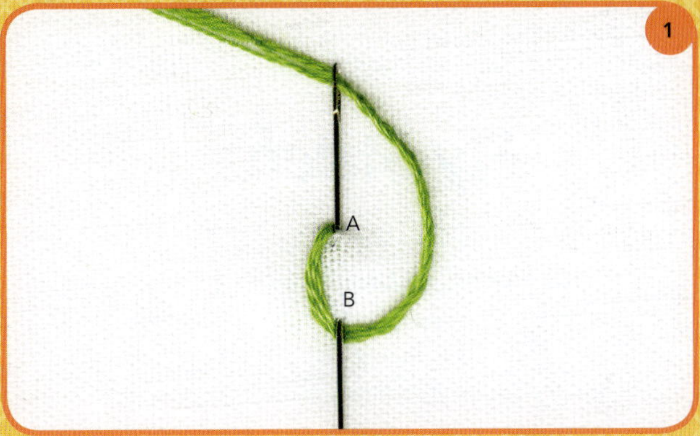

1

A

B

2

B   C

Lazy Daisy Stitch

Detached chain stitches arranged in a flower shape are known as lazy daisy stitches. You can keep them separate and fill the center with one or more French knots, or come up through the same hole in the center each time.

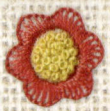

Fly Stitch

Fly stitches can be embroidered as standalone stitches or as a row of stitching. It is essentially an open detached chain stitch and is sometimes called a Y stitch because of its shape.

THE STEPS

1. Bring your thread to the front at point A. Stick the needle into the fabric at B and reemerge at C, with the thread lying under the tip of the needle. Pull the thread through until the V of the fly stitch lies flush against the emerging thread.

2. Secure the stitch by taking your needle back down at D.

3. To stitch a row of fly stitches, bring your needle back up at E and then take a stitch from F to D as you did for the first fly stitch. Take your thread back down at G to complete the second stitch. Continue in this way to the end of the row.

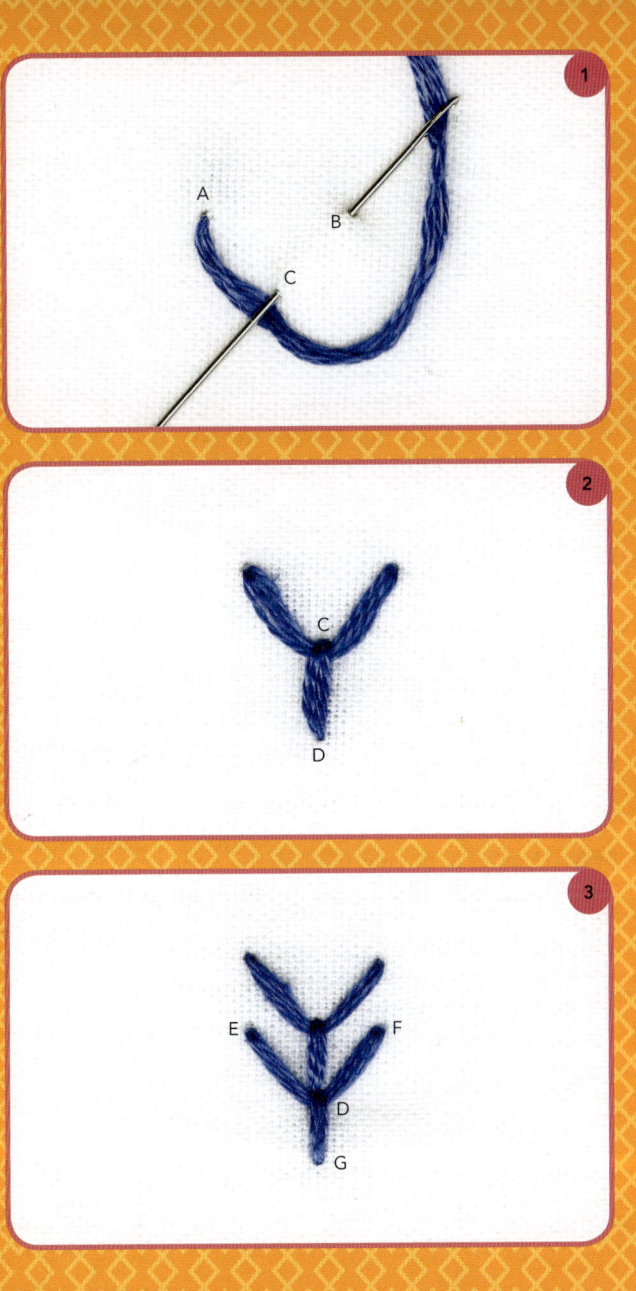

French Knot

Use a milliner/straw needle for knots. Traditionally, French knots were made by wrapping the thread around the needle just once, but today we tend to use more wraps. The French knots in this book are created by wrapping the thread around the needle twice.

THE STEPS

1. Bring your thread up at A. Hold your needle in one hand and wrap the thread over the needle twice with the other.

2. Hold the thread taut so the wraps don't slip off the end of the needle and twist it around to stick into your fabric at B—close to A, but not through the same hole. Pull the wraps of thread taut around the needle so that they lie against the fabric and—keeping hold of your thread so the wraps don't come loose—pull your needle through to the back, drawing the thread through the loops to create the knot.

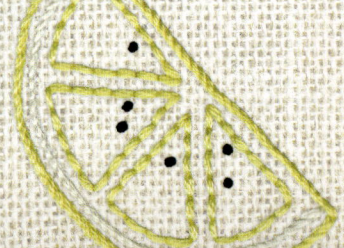

1

A

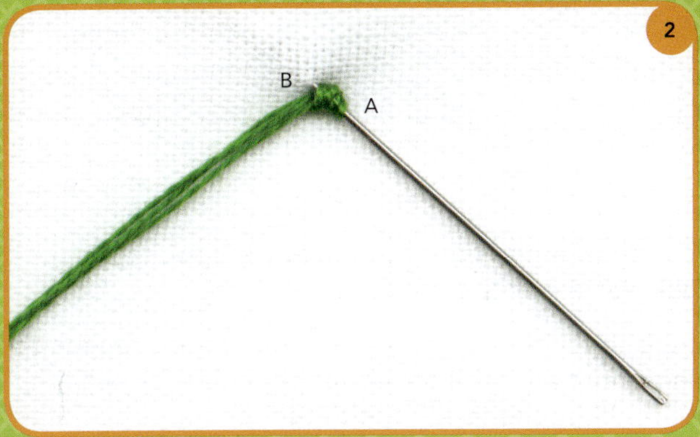

2

B   A

Pistil Stitch

A pistil stitch is basically a French knot with a tail, worked in the traditional way with just one wrap of thread. Points A and B are farther apart, but the stitch is worked in the same way (see the Planted Flower design on p. 60).

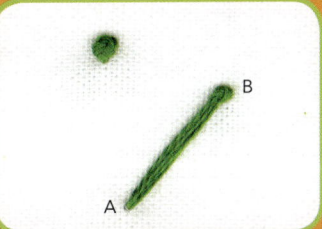

B

A

Running Stitch

Running stitch is a simple stitch that can be spaced in various ways to different effect. Bear in mind when creating your own designs that sections of any line drawn onto your fabric will show, as running stitch doesn't cover the line completely.

THE STEPS

1. Bring your thread up at A, then take your needle down at B and reemerge at C.

2. Continue in this way to the end of the row, taking your thread to the back of the fabric to complete the last stitch.

3. Experiment with different lengths of stitches and gaps to create various effects with running stitch.

Satin Stitch

Satin stitch fills an area with straight stitches. To do this, use a stab stitch: Bring your thread up through the fabric and take it down in two actions. Begin in the middle of the area you want to fill and stitch outward, then return to the center and fill the other half. The shape to be filled dictates the direction of your stitches. Follow any curves by increasing the space between stitches along one edge and decreasing on the other.

THE STEPS

1. Bring your thread to the front of the fabric at A and take it down again at B as you would to make a straight stitch. Come up again at C and take your thread to the back again at D to create the next stitch.

2. Continue in this way until the entire area is filled with dense stitching.

3. To embroider a satin stitch triangle (as in the Cozy Cottage and Morning Mug designs on p. 46 and p. 58), bring your thread up at A and take it down again at B. Come up at C and down at B, and continue in this way until the last stitch, where you'll come up in the center of the base of the triangle—point H—and take your thread down for the last time at B for a neat finish.

Star Stitch

Star stitch is an isolated stitch that can be scattered randomly over an area or worked in a grid pattern for a more uniform look. It can be caught down in the middle with a small cross-stitch, too, if you prefer.

THE STEPS

1. Come up at A. Stick your needle into the fabric at B and reemerge at C. Pull your thread through to make the first stitch.

2. Do the same from D to E and F to G, then take your thread to the back at H.

3. Complete the star stitch by catching it down with a small stitch from I to J.

Stem Stitch

Stem stitch is good for outlines. The trick is to bring your needle up through the hole at the end of the prior stitch, and to always keep your thread below your needle. Use even stitch lengths for a neat row. Done correctly, stem stitch forms a row of backstitch on the back of your work.

THE STEPS

1. Bring your thread up at A and, working from left to right, make the first stitch from B to A. Your thread should reemerge through the same hole at A.

2. Keep your thread below your needle at all times, and make the next stitch from C to B, bringing your needle up through the same hole at B. Continue stitching along the line in this way.

3. To end off a row of stem stitch, make the last stitch from D to C and then take the needle back down at D. You can omit this last half stitch and take your needle down straight at D when making the last stitch—using this method will leave a thinner section at the end of the row. For a closed shape such as a circle, make the last stitch from A to D, and then take your needle back down again at B (covering your first small stitch) to hide the join.

Projects

How-to Instructions

Smart Fox

Threads: black, light green, yellow, dark green, orange, and white

Body: Using four strands of orange, outline the body in a double row of stem stitch and embroider the legs in backstitch.

Tail: Make the tip of the tail with stem stitch using four strands of white. Outline the rest of the tail with stem stitch using four strands of orange.

Head: Use two strands of black to satin stitch the pupils of the eyes and the nose. Outline the face in stem stitch using four strands of orange for the lower half and four strands of white for the upper half. Outline the eyes in stem stitch with two strands of orange. Fill in the ears with satin stitch using three strands of white, and outline the head in stem stitch with four strands of orange.

Background: Embroider the lines in stem stitch. Use four strands of light green for the top two rows and embroider the second line as a double row. Use four strands of dark green for the bottom two rows and stitch the fourth line as a double row. Use four strands of yellow for the cross-stitches.

✳ *Tip: The direction in which your satin stitches lie will change the look of the finished design, so consider the various options before starting to stitch.*

Adorable Apple

Threads: salmon, light green, and dark green

Apple: Outline the apple in stem stitch using four strands of salmon. Embroider a second row of stem stitch inside the first, excluding the bite. Stitch the lines on the apple in backstitch with four strands of salmon. Embroider the crosses using four strands of light green and cross-stitch.

Stem and leaves: Embroider the stem using four strands of dark green and stem stitch. Outline the leaves in stem stitch with three strands of light green, then fill them in with detached chain stitches using three strands of dark green.

✳ Tip: If you struggle to get your backstitches the same length, try working it as a stab stitch or use a ruler to mark dots on the fabric at equal intervals to guide you.

Happy Bird

Threads: light salmon, light green, yellow, and white

Bird: Outline the bird in stem stitch using four strands of light salmon. Embroider the wing in chain stitch with three strands of light salmon and then whip the chain stitch using two strands of white. To create the flower, use two strands of light salmon to embroider in blanket stitch and then fill the center circle with French knots using three strands of yellow. Embroider the eye using two strands of light green and satin stitch.

Background: Embroider the top of the circle in French knots using four strands of yellow. Use three strands of yellow for the star stitches. For the sprigs of foliage, stitch with four strands of light green—use stem stitch for the stem and detached chain stitch for the leaves.

❋ *Tip: When doing whipped chain stitch, use one strand less for the whipping to give a nice and even, candy-striped look to the stitching.*

Cozy Cottage

Threads: salmon, dark blue, light blue, light green, yellow, dark green, orange, and white

Fence: Embroider the fence posts as long straight stitches using four strands of light green. Stitch the horizontal lines with four strands of dark green in backstitch, catching the straight stitches down. Space your stitching so that there's a stitch over each post and two stitches between each pair of posts.

Sky: Use two strands of thread and alternate between dark blue and light blue to embroider the satin stitch triangles.

House: Outline the house in stem stitch using four strands of yellow and the window using three strands of yellow. Embroider the window crossbars with two strands of white in satin stitch. Use three strands of light green and tiny backstitches to embroider the number three, and two strands of light green in satin stitch for the doorknob. Stitch the square around the number in backstitch with three strands of dark green, then outline the door in stem stitch using four strands of dark green.

Flowers: Embroider the stems with two strands of dark green in stem stitch. Working from left to right, create the first flower with detached chain stitches in three strands of white. Use two strands of orange and blanket stitch for the petals of the next flower, then fill the center with French knots using two strands of white. Create the next flower with French knots in three strands of orange. Embroider the fourth flower in the same way, but use white. Stitch the detached chain flower on the far right in two strands of orange.

Roof: Embroider the lower edge of the roof in blanket stitch using two strands of salmon. Keep the purl side of the stitching along the straight edge. Outline the rest of the roof in stem stitch using four strands of salmon. Embroider the chimney with backstitch in four strands of salmon. Using four strands of salmon, stitch the French knots scattered across the roof.

✳ *Tip: Change the length of your stitches to suit the design. Smaller backstitches for the door number work better than the bigger stitches used for the fence.*

Pretty Butterfly

Threads: salmon, light salmon, dark blue, light blue, light green, and yellow

Body and antennae: Use three strands of light blue and straight stitch to embroider the lines on the body, then outline it in stem stitch using three strands of dark blue. Start stitching the antennae at the bottom in three strands of dark blue and backstitch, and end with a detached chain stitch.

Upper wings: Embroider the flower in the left-hand wing with blanket stitch in three strands of yellow. Make the circles in the right-hand wing in French knots using two strands of yellow for the inner circle and three strands for the outer circle. Use three strands of salmon for the rows of fly stitch, then outline the upper wings in chain stitch with three strands of light salmon.

Lower wings: Outline the lower wings in two rows of stem stitch using four strands of light green for the inner row and three for the outer row. Stitch the smaller shape inside the wings in chain stitch using two strands of light blue. Stitch two additional rows inside the first.

Small butterflies: Embroider the left-hand butterfly in four strands of light blue. The wings are detached chain stitch and the antennae are pistil stitch. The right-hand butterfly is embroidered the same way, but using three strands of light green.

✳ *Tip: Vary the number of threads you use for French knots to create different textures. Use more strands of thread for bigger knots rather than additional wraps—your knots will look neater this way.*

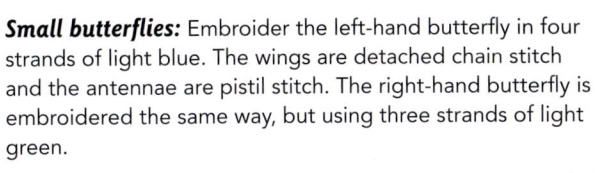

Friendly Fish

Threads: black, dark blue, light blue, light green, yellow, dark green, and white

Body: Outline the body of the fish in stem stitch using four strands of dark blue. Embroider the gills in backstitch with four strands of light blue and the eye as a blanket stitch pinwheel with an open center using two strands of black. Use four strands of dark green for the cross-stitches and three strands of light blue and star stitch to create the patterns on the fish.

Tail: Embroider the outer and inner lines with chain stitch. Use three strands of dark blue for the outer and two strands of light blue for the inner.

Fins: Outline both fins in stem stitch using four strands of light blue. Create the lines inside the fins in backstitch using three strands of dark blue.

Bubbles: The bubbles are blanket stitch pinwheels. Use two strands each of light green, yellow, and white, and the reference photo as a guide for color placement.

❋ *Tip: Switch between closed and open blanket stitch pinwheels to create interest or to suit your design.*

Embellished Flower

Threads: light salmon, light green, yellow, and white

Inner flower: Use two strands of yellow to embroider the center circle in satin stitch. Create the petals using blanket stitch, keeping the purl edge of the stitching on the inside and using two strands of yellow.

Outer petals: Embroider the circle in stem stitch using four strands of light salmon. Stitch another row just inside the first using three strands of light salmon. Use chain stitch and three strands of light salmon for the petals. The circle in each petal is a blanket stitch pinwheel in two strands of white.

Straight stitch flowers: Use straight stitch and three strands of light green for the flower on the left and two strands for the two on the right. Use three strands of yellow for the French knots in the center of each flower.

Leaves: Outline the leaves in stem stitch using four strands of light green. Embroider the fly stitch veins in three strands of light green.

❋ *Tip: Keep the purl edge of your blanket stitching on the inside rather than the outside line of a shape to give it a different look.*

Jolly Snowman

Threads: black, salmon, dark blue, light blue, light green, orange, and white

Snowflake: Use three strands of light blue to embroider the rows of fly stitch that make up the snowflake.

Background: Create the background lines with whipped chain stitch. Use three strands of light blue for the chain stitching and whip it with two strands of white.

Snowman

Hat: Embroider the band of the hat in satin stitch with two strands of light green. Outline the hat in stem stitch in black, using three strands for the top and four strands for the brim.

Scarf: Use three strands of salmon. Embroider the stripes in straight stitch and the outline in stem stitch.

Buttons: Embroider with satin stitch using two strands of black.

Body: Outline the snowman's body in a double row of stem stitch using four strands of white.

Arms: Embroider the twig arms in four strands of dark blue—use fly stitch for the ends of the twigs, and then carry on in backstitch for the stalks. Embroider the arm on the left over the stitching that outlines the body.

Carrot nose: Fill this in with satin stitch using two strands of orange, and angle the stitches to create a nice point at the end.

Head and face: Outline the head in stem stitch with four strands of white. Use six strands of black in French knots for the eyes. For the mouth, use three strands of black in French knots. Wrap the thread around the needle an extra time for the three knots in the center to make them bigger than the two outer knots.

✳ *Tip: Combine stitches to create the look you want, such as fly and backstitch for the snowman's twig arms.*

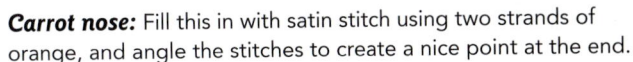

Lovely Heart

Threads: salmon, light salmon, light green, yellow, dark green, and white

Main heart: Embroider the vertical lines in backstitch using four strands of salmon. Outline the heart in whipped chain stitch—use three strands of salmon for the chain stitching and two strands of white for the whipping. Stitch the outer heart in stem stitch with four strands of salmon. Embroider the circles as blanket stitch pinwheels using two strands of white.

Small heart: Outline the small heart using stem stitch with three strands of light salmon. Embroider the French knot flowers in two strands of light salmon.

Flower: Fill the center circle with satin stitch using two strands of yellow and embroider the outer circle in stem stitch with three strands of yellow. Using three strands of light green, stitch the lines inside each petal in backstitch and the background petals in stem stitch. Use four strands of dark green to stem stitch the full petals.

✳ *Tip: Play around with the positioning and number of French knots to create different small flowers.*

Morning Mug

Threads: salmon, light salmon, dark blue, light blue, light green, yellow, dark green, and orange

Mug: Embroider the rim of the mug in stem stitch, using two strands of light green for the inside edge and three strands of dark green for the outer edge. Outline the mug in four strands of light green in stem stitch. Use three strands for the inside edge of the handle. Create the two lines at the base of the mug using backstitch of four strands of dark green. Embroider the zigzag line in backstitch with four strands of dark blue. Stitch all three spirals of steam in stem stitch—use two strands of light blue for the left-hand spiral, three strands of light green for the middle, and two strands of dark blue for the right-hand spiral. Embroider the French knot dots on the mug using two strands of light blue.

Border: Embroider the satin stitch triangles using two strands of thread. Start with salmon, stitch the next triangle in orange, followed by yellow, and then light salmon. Repeat the colors in this sequence all the way around the circle.

✳ *Tip: Save the knots for last so they don't get squashed in the hoop if you need to move it around.*

Planted Flower

Threads: salmon, light green, yellow, dark green, and orange

Flower: Embroider a backstitch trellis in the center of the flower using four strands of yellow. Try not to split the thread at the intersections. Use two strands of orange to embroider the circles in chain stitch. Create the petals with stem stitch using four strands of salmon.

Stem and leaves: Outline the leaves in stem stitch using four strands of dark green. Embroider the central leaf vein in backstitch and the side veins in pistil stitch using four strands of dark green. Make two rows of stem stitch back to back using four strands of dark green to create the flower stem.

Background: Embroider the background in running stitch with four strands of light green.

✳ *Tip: Use a stab stitch technique for the trellis. Bring the needle up and down in two separate movements to create the backstitches.*

Charming Raccoon

Threads: black, salmon, light green, yellow, and white

Body: Outline the body in stem stitch using four strands of black. Make the legs with backstitch using four strands of black.

Tail: Fill each section of the tail with satin stitch using three strands and alternating between black and white. Position the stitches so they follow the curve of the tail.

Head and face: Use two strands of black and satin stitch for the nose and pupils of the eyes. Outline the eyes in three strands of black in stem stitch. Embroider the lower half of the face in stem stitch of four strands of white. Use two strands of white and satin stitch for the ears. Outline the rest of the face and head in stem stitch using four strands of black.

Border: Create the flowers using detached chain stitches in three strands of thread. Start on the lower left with salmon, then use yellow, light green, and yellow again. Repeat the sequence around the circle of flowers.

✳ *Tip: Stitch the detached chains in pairs of opposites rather than moving from one to the next around the circle. This will prevent the thread from building up unevenly in the center.*

About the Author

Kelly Fletcher is a largely self-taught hand embroiderer who grew up among needles, thread, yarn and fabric. Working in the media and advertising industry gave her the remaining skills she needed to begin creating original patterns, which she sells online. Kelly's style can be described as contemporary creative surface embroidery. She draws on traditional stitches and techniques, but puts a contemporary spin on them to create fresh designs that appeal to the modern embroiderer. She has contributed to various publications and books, more about which can be found at www.kellyfletcher.co.za.